Turning hay at the Weald & Downland Open Air Museum, Singleton, West Sussex. Pete Betsworth is using a Shire gelding and a Lister Blackstone swath-turner.

Heavy Horses

Diana Zeuner

D0324664

Shire Publications

For Chris Zeuner, dearly loved husband and friend,
who introduced us both to heavy horses.

Published in 2004 by Shire Publications Ltd,
Cromwell House, Church Street, Princes Risborough,
Buckinghamshire HP27 9AA, UK.
(Website: www.shirebooks.co.uk)

British Library Cataloguing in Publication Data:
Zeuner, Diana
Heavy horses. – (Shire album; 431)
1. Draft horses
I. Title
636.1'5
ISBN 0 7478 0602 0

Cover: *Shire horses Truman and Josh, owned by Rob Dash of Dunsfold, Surrey, pause during a ploughing match in West Sussex.*

ACKNOWLEDGEMENTS
The author is indebted to the very many people throughout the heavy horse world whose knowledge and help over many years have contributed to this book. They include especially: Carl Boyde MRCVS; Tom Brewster; Rob Dash; Mike Flood, Angela and Richard Gifford; Edward Hart; Terry Keegan; Rowena and John McDermott; Geoff Morton; John Peacock; Charlie Pinney; Nick Rayner; Philip Ryder-Davies MB, BS, BVSc, MRCVS; John Ward; John Zawadzki.
  Photographs are acknowledged as follows: Bath and North East Somerset Community Recycling, page 43 (top); courtesy of Richard Beard, pages 7 (top), 9 (bottom right), 38; Bracknell Forest Borough Council, page 42 (bottom); Bernard Chambers, page 34 (bottom); Coors Visitor Centre, page 44 (bottom right); Hilary Cotter, pages 9 (top), 40 (top), 44 (top left), 45; Gary Crisp, page 17; W. L. Easton, page 13 (bottom); Paul Felix, page 50 (top right); Roy Fox, pages 8 (top and bottom), 9 (bottom left), 12 (right), 16 (top and centre), 18 (bottom), 24, 26 (top and bottom), 29 (bottom two), 43 (centre and bottom), 60 (bottom); John Fraser, page 13 (top); Colin Fry Collection, Museum of English Rural Life, pages 41 (top), 56; courtesy of Duncan Gillespie, pages 7 (centre), 14, 32 (bottom), 34 (top); Eric Guy Collection, Museum of English Rural Life, pages 31 (both), 32 (top two), 33 (centre), 49; Donald Hanson Shire Horse Archive, Keith Chivers Bequest, Museum of English Rural Life, pages 7 (bottom), 8 (centre), 11 (upper left), 33 (bottom), 44 (centre); Audrey Hart, page 6; Heavy Horse World archive, pages 4, 10, 12 (left), 15 (both), 22, 34 (centre), 35 (top), 36 (bottom), 50 (top left), 54 (centre and bottom), 58 (bottom), 59 (bottom); Horses at Work, Bradford Industrial Museum, page 42 (top); Institute of Agricultural History and Museum of English Rural Life, University of Reading, pages 18 (top), 33 (top), 48 (top), 51 (both); the Liverpool Carters Association, page 37; Colleen Mowbray, pages 19 (top), 47 (bottom); Clarence Naylor, page 28 (both); John Peacock, page 40 (bottom); Charlie Pinney, pages 35 (bottom), 55 (top); Bob Powell, page 46 (centre right); Rob Rawstorne, page 36 (top); Brian Robinson, page 20 (bottom); Shire Horse Society, pages 11 (right), 38; Jeff Smith, page 39 (bottom); Kate Stephen, page 48 (bottom); Suffolk Horse Society, page 59 (top); Suffolk Punch Horse Museum, page 16 (bottom); M. Wight Collection, Museum of English Rural Life, page 50 (bottom); courtesy of Wisbech Shire Horse Society, page 11 (bottom); courtesy of Frank Yardley, page 20 (top); Young's Brewery, Wandsworth, page 39 (top); Diana Zeuner, pages 1, 21 (both), 23, 26 (centre), 27 (both), 29 (top two), 30 (both), 41 (bottom), 44 (top right and bottom left), 46 (top, centre left and bottom), 47 (top), 52 (all), 53 (both), 54 (top), 55 (bottom three), 57 (top), 58 (both), 60 (top), 61; Francesca Zeuner, page 19 (bottom).
'The Horse' on page 3 is reproduced by permission of the Ronald Duncan Literary Foundation.

Printed in Malta by Gutenberg Press Limited, Gudja Road, Tarxien PLA 19, Malta.

Contents

The Horse

Where in this wide world can man find nobility without pride, friendship without envy or beauty without vanity? Here, where grace is laced with muscle, and strength by gentleness confined.

He serves without servility; he has fought without enmity. There is nothing so powerful, nothing less violent, there is nothing so quick, nothing more patient.

England's past has been borne on his back. All our history is his industry; we are his heirs, he our inheritance.

Ronald Duncan

Glossary

Action: the way a horse moves.

Breaking in: the process of training a young horse.

Clean-legged: horses without *feather*.

Colt: a young uncastrated male horse.

Feather: the silky hair around the feet of Shires, Clydesdales and some native ponies.

Filly: a young female horse.

Flights: decorations (for showing purposes) usually made of wire and ribbon and threaded into a raffia or wool plait along the mane and at the top of the tail.

Gelding: a castrated male horse.

'Good doers': horses that keep fit and well without the need for much extra food.

Grey: the name given to a grey or white horse.

Hames: curved lengths of wood, metal, or a combination of the two, which are fixed into a runnel on the collar and, fitted with attachment hooks and rings, enable a horse to be coupled to a vehicle or implement.

Hand: a unit of measurement used to indicate the height of a horse (originally measured by the width of a man's hand) – about 4 inches (10 cm).

'Hard' feed: cereal-based feed used to supplement grass and hay.

Hitch cart: a modern small two-wheeled cart with seat that is hitched to the horse in front and to an implement behind to facilitate a more efficient task.

Pasterns: the first (long) and second (short) phalanges of the forelimb and the joint formed there, just above the hoof.

Stallion: a male horse that is entire (uncastrated) and able to breed.

Stud book: a book recording all registered animals of a particular breed.

Traces: trace chains (sometimes leather or rope) that are attached to the *hames* at the front of the horse and to an implement or vehicle at the rear.

Whipple tree: a length of metal or wood attached to a farm implement to which the *traces* from the horse's collar are fastened, joining the horse to the implement.

A stocky woodsman's horse, probably a stallion, with a showy mane, thought to have been photographed in the early 1900s. Thousands of such horses were at work in draught all over Britain alongside their heavier brethren.

Introduction

In the hearts of many people throughout the developed world there is a very special place for heavy draught horses. Before the advent of steam and the internal combustion engine, and as ox draught came to an end, Western economies were entirely dependent on the horse for traction, in town and countryside. The horse (and especially the heavy draught horse) played a pivotal role in the industrial and agricultural revolutions in Britain, toiling in mines and quarries, at mills, factories and docks, alongside canals and railway lines, in fields and pasture, working in partnership with the fashionable new technologies.

At the dawn of the twentieth century there were some 2.6 million horses in agriculture and trade; in 1920 1,440,948 of these were heavy draught horses. A survey in 1986, carried out with some difficulty in view of the changed nature of draught-horse activity, found only some ten thousand.

The two world wars reduced the numbers of heavy draught horses dramatically – both through conflict and their replacement by the tractor and the motor lorry. By the 1950s draught horses had reached an all-time low, with some heavy breeds near extinction. The upsurge of interest in Britain's heritage in the 1960s and 1970s led to a revival in the fortunes of heavy horses as enthusiasts gathered at ploughing matches and agricultural shows to admire their majestic appearance and their qualities of strength and endurance.

Heavy horses – Shires from England, Clydesdales from Scotland and the Borders, Suffolk Punches from East Anglia and British Percherons – epitomised a way of life that was slipping from grasp, that was considered worth celebrating and continuing, and, most important, developing in a new way for the future.

In the twenty-first century, with agriculture undergoing enormous changes and promotional work in towns decreasing, the heavy horse nevertheless holds its head high. In Britain, Europe, the United States, Canada, Australia and New Zealand determined individuals are breeding, showing and working heavy draught horses and encouraging newcomers and fresh sport activity, such as cross-country driving, ensuring a place for 'heavies' in a high-tech world.

The breeds and breeding

In the twenty-first century the breeding of pedigree heavy draught horses remains chiefly in the hands of the small group of farmers who carried on through the low years of the 1950s and 1960s, and their sons and daughters. Many also judge at agricultural shows, their knowledge and experience often stretching back several generations.

Much has changed since their forefathers bred horses for the lucrative town market, keeping the lesser specimens for work at home on the land. Stallions would be 'walked' to mares at local farms: today greater mobility means that mare owners are prepared to travel many miles to make use of a suitable, or fashionable, stallion. Increasingly use is being made of AI (artificial insemination), and chilled or frozen semen, which means that a stallion in Lincolnshire can father a colt or filly in the United States or Australia.

Breeding pedigree draught horses to ensure good-quality animals for work was once a necessity. It was also very fashionable – even King George V did it, winning frequent prizes. By 2004 demand was comparatively limited and prices variable. Nevertheless, new owners continue to enter the heavy horse sector and enthusiastic new breeders are eagerly sought by the breed societies. Numbers of Suffolk and Clydesdale horses are particularly low and these breeds are officially regarded as rare under the Rare Breeds Survival Trust's criteria: ensuring a bright future for them requires active promotion. Cross-breeding using a heavy horse sire and a light horse dam,

Judging a Percheron in-hand class. Knowledge of heavy horse confor-mation and character is often passed on through many generations.

Until after the Second World War stallions would be brought early in the season to special parades and fairs at which farmers could choose a stallion to serve their mares. This photograph was taken in the centre of Penistone, South Yorkshire, in 1907.

Stallions were walked from farm to farm within the area in which they were servicing mares. Some of the stallion walkers, who spent weeks away from home with their charges, developed similar reputations to those of their stallions! This illustration shows R. O. Watson's Clydesdale, Ability, who travelled central Orkney in 1915. With him is staigyman (stallion walker) Robbie Couper.

W. H. Neale's Shire stallion, Coleshill Brilliant King, stud book number 28215, who travelled the Nailstone area of Leicestershire, with James Boulstridge, waggoner to Warner Barr. The photograph was taken in 1915.

Trelow Father Abraham, bred by Terry Sandling in Cornwall in 1990, made Shire breed history by providing frozen semen for a pioneering global breeding project. In 1999 he was exported to Australia to boost the country's Shire blood-lines.

King George V, a prominent breeder of Shire horses, collects the Shire Horse Society's Gold Challenge Cup in 1921 from Mr A. C. Duncombe at the national breed show. His self-bred Field Marshall V (pictured on page 11) was a multiple breed champion in the 1920s.

The Suffolk horse is one of the rarest equine breeds in the world, with only about eighty breeding females remaining, most of them still in Suffolk. Stalwart efforts are being made by the Suffolk Horse Society to reverse the breed's fortunes. In the photograph Dorset breeder Randy Hiscock is showing his five-year-old champion mare Donhead Hall Alexandra at the New Forest Show in 1998.

Small, stocky horses with good temperaments are still sought by people keen to work their animals. This mare was worked regularly in the forests in the late 1990s and is wearing an American collar, favoured by many modern horsemen.

usually to produce a heavy hunter or driving horse for leisure, can be a useful source of extra income for the breeder.

Modern conformation of a heavy draught horse is different from that preferred in the past. In the days when heavy horses were the engines of industry they were bred for strength and stamina. In the twenty-first century the chief market is leisure. For appearance in the show ring, as a driven horse in promotional draught teams and for competitive sport, a leaner, less sturdy horse is frequently the aim. The modern Shire, therefore, is taller, has a narrower chest, less width of bone and less 'feather' on its feet than its predecessor, partly through cross-breeding with the slightly lighter Clydesdale. This is a development frowned upon by many heavy horse supporters, from both the older generation and the younger working horsemen.

A modern show horse compared with a working animal from the late nineteenth century. (Left) Philip Moss's champion Shire stallion Walton Supreme. Note the fine feather on the legs – an 'improvement' of modern times – and the expertly plaited mane complete with 'flights' or ' standards' to accentuate the stallion's crest. (Right) Spark, a black Shire stallion bred in 1878 by William Rowland, of Creslow, Buckinghamshire. This horse was champion at the London Show (the equivalent of today's National Shire Horse Show) in 1881, 1882 and 1883. The animal had the renowned stallion Honest Tom on his mother's side. This stallion was the first well-publicised private purchase of Walter Gilbey, of the gin-producing family.

The elegant modern Shire with its flamboyant style is much sought after in Europe. Here, in Fernwald, Germany, Ben Arnold is riding his animal imported from the United Kingdom.

There remains a market for smaller versions of heavy breeds – those who work their horses on the land or in the forests still require animals with good draught abilities and find their stockier heavy horses among those not destined for the show ring.

Many British breeders have found an important market for their animals overseas. Since the nineteenth century Clydesdales have been exported to Canada, the United States and Australasia. Shires have long been sought in the United States, and in the early twentieth century Suffolks were also exported, again to the United States in particular. Since the early 1990s Europe, especially Germany, France and the Netherlands, has provided a new market, particularly for Shires, and there are strong affiliated breed associations in those countries.

THE SHIRE

The most numerous and familiar of the heavy horse breeds in Britain, the Shire is a (rather distant) descendant of the Great Horse, used in medieval warfare and later improved by crossing the largest of the native horses with heavy horses imported from Flanders and Holland. When heavy plate armour disappeared lighter horses were used in preference and heavy horses found a valuable niche in agriculture, where they gradually replaced the slower oxen. By the mid eighteenth century the Black Horse, a type of Great Horse, was prevalent in the Midlands. The best-known animal from this period is the Packington Blind Horse, whose descendants were bred in Leicestershire.

Towards the end of the nineteenth century the Shire breed was booming. Lincolnshire Lad II, foaled in 1872, sired many winners in the show ring, including the famous Harold, foaled in 1881 and champion at the London Show in 1887. The English Cart Horse stud book had been started in 1878, when the horse was found predominantly from the Humber to the Cam and westwards to Cheshire and parts of Lancashire and adjoining counties. Six years later the name of the breed was changed to 'Shire' and the first volume of the stud book contained the records of 2381 stallions, some dating back to 1770. The popularity of the Shire spread to the United States; between 1900 and 1918 some four thousand Shires were exported there.

During the Second World War thousands of Shires were slaughtered and some of the largest stud farms, including the Forshaws' at Carlton-on-Trent, closed completely. At the 1955 Spring Show there were only twenty-six stallions, twenty-eight mares and fourteen geldings exhibited.

In the 1960s the East of England Agricultural Society's secretary, Roy Bird, was given the task of closing down the Shire Horse Society. Heavy horses were at their lowest ebb and to some there seemed little point in continuing the society's work. However, it was not in Roy Bird's nature to give up and over the next few years, aided by a small group of determined breeders and brewers keen on the Shire, he set about building up interest in Britain's most numerous group of heavy horses.

At an early stage Roy Bird was joined in the endeavour by a retired headmaster, Keith Chivers, who was to develop his interest to the extent of becoming the Shire breed's official historian, writing the seminal work *The Shire Horse* (J. A. Allen, 1977) and developing the Shire Horse Archive. This was deposited on his death in 1998 with the Museum of English Rural Life at the University of Reading. Apart from the resolute task performed by Shire breeders, these two men did more than anyone to ginger enthusiasm and thus ensure the survival not only of the Shire breed but of all heavy horses.

The Shire breed's fortunes revived during the 1970s and 1980s and new export markets were established overseas. The first World Shire Congress was held at Peterborough in March 1996. The Shire is not a rare breed although it is considered a 'minority' breed, and ardent breed followers have expressed concern about the decreasing number of mares, with the implications of fewer foals and reduced blood-lines.

Shire Horse Society secretary Roy Bird in the foreground, with the society's president for 1988, His Royal Highness the Duke of Edinburgh, and, from left, deputy presidents Charles Tidbury and J. Yerburgh at that year's Shire Horse Show.

Keith Chivers, the Shire breed's historian, at work at his home near Bristol.

During the heyday of the working horse there was much greater emphasis on breeding for efficient draught power. This meant a horse with bigger 'bone', strong front and rear quarters and shorter legs. This is King George V's stallion Field Marshall V in 1920 when he was Shire Show Champion. Societies such as the Wisbech Shire Horse Society (founded in 1903) were formed to hire stallions of choice to breed with the mares of society members.

Brothers Paul and Walt Bedford's York-based Deighton stud dominated the Shire showing and breeding scene throughout the 1980s and 1990s and into the first years of the twenty-first century. (Left) The celebrated mare Landcliffe Laura, National Shire Horse of the Year Champion for four years running (1985–8), seen at the Horse of the Year Show at Wembley Arena in 1988. (Right) The stamp of mare that the Bedford brothers are consummate at turning out: this is Deighton Deborah at the Great Yorkshire Show in 2002.

The Shire is known for its equable temperament, strong character and courageous nature. Colours are black, brown, bay or grey. Stallions should stand from 17.2 hands and weigh up to 2464 pounds (1118 kg) when mature.

THE CLYDESDALE

The Clydesdale is Scotland's indigenous heavy breed, taking its name and its *c*.1700 origins from the upper reaches of the river Clyde. Clyde Valley farmers developed a breed capable of drawing 20–30 cwt (907–1361 kg) in a single cart at a pace of $3^1/2$–5 mph (6–8 km/h) at a walk. To achieve this, springiness of stride was needed, which was obtained through breeding for well-sloped pasterns and big, sound feet.

It was not until 1877 that the Clydesdale Horse Society of Great Britain and Ireland was established to promote the breed and maintain its purity. Two successful stallions of the late nineteenth century were Darnley and Prince of Wales. Hiawatha and Baron's Pride followed, the latter owned by A. and W. Montgomery, proprietors of the Netherhall Stud, until 1918 the biggest and most influential Clydesdale stud in the world. In 1920 the stud book for the breed held a record number of entries – 6870. Most important of the three hundred stallions listed that year was Fyvie Sensation, sire of the 1926 Cawdor Cup winner Benefactor, arguably one of the greatest stallions in the breed's history.

The legendary Baron of Buchlyvie was the most expensive stallion of all time. Bred by William McKeitch of Buchlyvie, he sold at Ayr Mart on 14th December 1911 for £9500 (the equivalent of £600,000 in 2004) to William Dunlop, with whom he was in dispute and who already had a half share in the horse. Baron's son Dunure Footprint (1908–30) won every

Collessie Cut Above, one of the most influential modern Clydesdale stallions, was bred by Ronnie Black of Ladybank, Cupar, Fife. The stallion and his progeny have collected trophies wherever shown.

trophy available and is reputed to have sired more foals than any other Clydesdale stallion. One year 146 of his foals were registered.

In 2004 the Clydesdale Horse Society had some 900 members and around 350 registered breeders, registering around 150 foals a year. The breed enjoys particular popularity not only in Scotland, northern England

Working Clydesdales. These are Robin Worthington's pair Rosie and Jim, seen here ploughing at Beamish, the North of England Open Air Museum, representing the sort of 'work-fit' Clydesdales that were once commonplace on farms in the Scottish Lowlands and northern England.

The legendary Clydesdale stallion Baron of Buchlyvie, who holds the record for the highest price ever paid for a British draught horse.

and Northern Ireland but also in the United States, Canada, Australia and New Zealand. Clydesdale driving teams of four or more horses are popular in North America and many of the best breeding animals are exported there for this purpose.

Alert yet docile, the Clydesdale, out of all the British heavy breeds, is particularly noted for its action, being slightly faster and lighter than its counterparts. Preferred colours today are dark brown or bay with a white stripe on the face and white legs to just over the knees and hocks. Chestnuts, blacks, light bays and roans are not uncommon. The Clydesdale's feather is traditionally silkier than that of the Shire, although in the modern animals there is little difference.

THE SUFFOLK PUNCH

The Suffolk horse is thought to be the oldest existing breed to retain its original appearance. It has the oldest breed society in England (founded in 1877) and the longest unbroken written pedigree of any breed of horse in the world. In the sixteenth century William Camden wrote in his *Britannia* of the native breed of working cart-horse in the eastern counties, a description that is easily recognisable as the present-day Suffolk.

It took two hundred years to create an agricultural horse that was perfect for farming tasks. In 1880 the first secretary of the Suffolk Horse Society, Herman Biddell, produced a stud book considered one of the finest ever written on livestock history. His researches revealed written pedigrees back to a stallion called Crisp's Horse of Ufford, foaled in 1768. This was not the first Suffolk horse, but the only male line remaining at this time: the others had died out. Another genetic bottleneck occurred at the end of the eighteenth century, when further lines died out. Inbreeding has continued to be popular among Suffolk breeders, concentrating useful characteristics, as well as less useful ones, in the current population.

Before the First World War there were thousands of Suffolk horses in East Anglia. Harness was characterised by wooden hames and saddles with exposed wooden trees, and larger farms with many working horses housed them at night in straw yards with shelters, as for cattle – an unusual arrangement for draught horses in England. Suffolks worked for very long periods without breaks – the standard working day in East Anglia in the winter was from 6.30 a.m. to 2.30 p.m. Regular journeys by commercial horses on the roads were of astounding lengths, perhaps as far as 25–30 miles (40–48 km).

After the Second World War it was not uncommon for large farms to sell off thirty or forty Suffolks in a single day: such was the glut on the market that the horses' fate was to be sold to the slaughterman. By 1966 only nine foals were registered. But for the determination of no more than half a dozen breeders, the Suffolk would have become extinct. However, renewed determination by the Suffolk Horse Society to encourage new owners and greater interest in the breed has been successful. A notable role was played by writer and broadcaster Paul Heiney, whose efforts at farming with horses – with the advice of prominent Suffolk horse farmers Roger Clark and Cheryl Grover – resulted in a huge increase in publicity for the breed. Dorset breeder Randy Hiscock pursued his search for fresh but traditional genes in the United States and in 2002 brought a Suffolk colt back across the Atlantic.

Right: Suffolks belonging to breeder Pauline Hutchinson of Haughley, Suffolk, taking part in the Suffolk breed show in 1978, when the heavy horse revival was in full swing. The three horses, Old Bells Greta, Old Bells Gwen and stallion Parham Rupert, took the show's Centenary Cup.

A fine line-up of Suffolk horses at a breed show in the 1980s.

Senior Suffolk stallion and supreme champion 2002, Mr B. Gillings's Golden Grandchild. Note the horse's punchy appearance and shorter, sturdier legs than those of the Shire or Clydesdale. This photograph also demonstrates the superb braiding (or plaiting) skills of Suffolk owners, using traditional bass (or raffia) and incorporating the whole of the mane and tail.

Her Majesty's Prison Hollesley Bay Colony is one of the largest Suffolk studs in the world. Here the stud's horseman Bruce Smith drives the prison's team of four to a dray supplied by Suffolk enthusiast Paul Rackham at the East of England Show in 1998.

In the twenty-first century the Suffolk Punch is one of the rarest breeds of horse in the world, and with only around eighty breeding females it is considered 'critical' under the Rare Breeds Survival Trust's criteria.

The Suffolk is always chesnut (traditionally spelled without the first 't') in colour, with shades varying from lemon through to a dark liver. The only white allowed is on the face. The Suffolk is easily recognisable by its very large body on relatively short legs, giving the horse its strength. It has no feather on the legs, has good hard feet and a docile and tractable temperament. Preferred heights are 17.2 hands for a stallion and 16.2 hands for a mare.

A typical top-quality Suffolk stallion from the early years of the twentieth century, this is Morston Gold King, 5643, bred by Arthur Pratt of Morston Hall, Felixstowe, by Morston Gold Guard, 4234, out of Leda's Queen, 7772, and foaled in 1924. He is pictured here at the age of four when he belonged to Mrs Evelyn Rich of Wretham Hall, Thetford, Norfolk.

THE BRITISH PERCHERON

The Percheron is one of the oldest and most internationally dispersed breeds in the world. French chroniclers trace it back to 732 when Charles Martel defeated the Saracens at Poitiers, claimed the horses as spoils of war and distributed them throughout France, particularly in the Perche district of Normandy. Rotrou, Count of Perche, also brought home stallions from the Crusades and crossed them with local mares to improve the stock of the Norman war-horses.

Among the horses brought to England by William, Duke of Normandy, in 1066 there may well have been some from the Perche region. In 1188 Giraldus Cambrensis mentioned 'many excellent studs set apart for breeding in Powys, all originating from Robert de Belleme's Percheron stallions', imported to his Welsh estates in 1098. These were not necessarily of a particular breed, and although the modern Percheron may owe some characteristics to the war-horses of the Middle Ages, it has changed considerably.

The first Percherons to be seen in any numbers in Britain were used to pull buses in large cities during the last quarter of Victoria's reign. Thomas Tilling, the London jobmaster, imported grade (cross-bred) Percherons from the United States (in 1896 he owned 3386 horses). The Americans had been importing quality French stock since the 1830s and used the stallions to improve the local draught mares, resulting in cross-breds being exported in their thousands.

The British Army also bought horses from Tilling. In 1900 he sold the Army a consignment of 325 horses, which were shipped out to South Africa and used in the Boer War. During the First World War the qualities of the Percheron as a heavy draught horse were particularly appreciated by the British Army – especially its absence of leg feather in the muddy wartime conditions, its calm nature and its ability to trot fast. The Ministry of Agriculture imported two pure-bred stallions and twelve mares in the autumn of 1916 and the following

The versatile Percheron proved to be ideal for breaking new ground in heavy horse activity. The Sampson and McDermott families from Hampshire provide a dramatic show-ring demonstration with their steam-driven fire engine drawn at speed by a pair of Percherons. In the display a fire is extinguished in a re-enactment of a real inferno from the horse-drawn era. This photograph was taken during their visit to France.

Limon, a champion Percheron stallion imported from France by Chivers & Sons Ltd in the early 1930s. Legs were shorter and bone was denser than in modern stallions of the breed.

year Sir William Birkbeck, Director of Remounts, imported a further twelve stallions and thirty-three mares. Between 1918 and 1922 thirty-six stallions and 321 mares were imported from France.

The British Percheron Horse Society was formed in 1918 to enable the registration and pro-motion of the breed. In the United Kingdom in 2004 there were some three hundred pure-bred Percherons (in France there were around five thousand). British Percheron enthusiasts continue to import them from France (between four and ten a year) and occasionally from Canada.

British Percherons have always been relatively low in numbers by virtue of being an import, but their fortunes can easily be improved by the buying in of animals from France and Canada. A number of breeders have introduced new blood in this way, while others using Percherons for leisure have also turned to these countries for animals of a particular type. In Hampshire the McDermott and Sampson families spearheaded the new sport of heavy horse cross-country driving trials with their Percheron horses, once again demonstrating the breed's renowned versatility.

Most Percherons are born black but the majority turn grey as they grow older. A black Percheron is born a dark dun colour and after shedding its foal coat remains black for the rest of its life. British Percheron stallions should exceed 16.3 hands (in the United States and Canada they are bred taller, while in France two types are recognised, one under 16 hands and the other over this height). Their good-natured temperament and general lack of nervous tension make them easy to train and work and ideal for the hobby enthusiast as well as the experienced horseman.

Gordon Bailey's celebrated British Percheron mare Willingham Phoebe was the dam of many winners and driving geldings in the late twentieth and early twenty-first century. During her life she collected over fifty championships. Her prize-winning foals were sired by Ryan's Day Granitdier, a Canadian horse imported by Jim Young.

The Working Horse Trust's Ardennes horses harrowing as a team of four at the Southern Counties Heavy Horse Association's spring working in 1999. The Ardennes is favoured as a shorter, stockier working type and now has its own breed society in the United Kingdom.

OTHER BREEDS USED IN DRAUGHT

Increasingly popular in Britain is the stocky Ardennes horse from a triangle of wooded hills in eastern France, southern Belgium and Luxembourg. Julius Caesar praised its quality and used the breed for heavy cavalry work. Many Ardennes reached the Holy Land during the Crusades, and the French and Belgian armies used them to haul artillery until after the First World War.

The Ardennes has been used extensively to found or improve other local breeds, such as the Auxois and Comtois, and a version of the breed is established in Sweden, where it is in demand as a forestry horse. Its qualities of strength, thriftiness, longevity and good temperament have endeared it to increasing numbers of British enthusiasts, and it is the anchor breed for the Working Horse Trust's working farm in East Sussex.

Some enthusiasts of the working horse prefer to use cross-bred animals with some heavy horse blood, or native ponies. These are often just as

Carl Boyde's coloured Percheron cross-bred waits by the horsebox at a spring working. Heavy crosses are popular with horse loggers and smallholders.

Frank Yardley's pair of coloured Cobs, heavy enough to do an excellent job of any agricultural task set for them. Their grandmothers were Clydesdales, their grandfather a coloured Cob, their mothers were half-bred Clydesdales and their father a coloured Cob of 15.2 hands. This photograph was taken at Hilltop Farm in Hainworth, Keighley, West Yorkshire, in 1982.

effective, especially because modern tasks are lighter than those in the heyday of the heavy draught horse, and because such animals can be cheaper to buy and keep. Historically they were of equal use to heavy horses, especially in the more remote parts of Britain.

The Vanner was a light cart-horse, a type rather than a breed, bred from a heavy mare and a lighter stallion or a cart-horse stallion and a native-breed mare. Standing at 14.1–15.1 hands, the Vanner was especially useful in the delivery trades, perhaps for a milkman or a greengrocer. This type can often be found at the fairs at Stow-on-the-Wold, Gloucestershire; Appleby, Cumbria; and Lee, Wakefield.

The Cleveland Bay, now listed as rare by the Rare Breeds Survival Trust, was at one time unrivalled as a coaching horse but was also used extensively on the land in the north-east of England. Its foundation was the Chapman horse (so called because it carried the wares of chapmen, the travelling salesmen of their day). Andalucian and Barb horse blood was also used to create the Cleveland, producing a powerful, clean-legged horse able to work heavy clay land and haul large loads, as well as carry men out hunting.

Native ponies, such as the Highland, Fell, Dales, Welsh Cob, Dartmoor, Exmoor, New Forest, Connemara, Irish Draught and Shetland, have all been used for draught and are highly suited to it. Donkeys and mules are less frequently seen in draught in Britain but are used extensively overseas.

Derek Marsden's Dales ponies successfully compete with heavy plough horses at ploughing matches.

Working and showing heavy horses

Heavy horses were developed for very specific roles and, although they share many characteristics with lighter horses, their care, management and work involve a wide range of specific skills. Once the new enthusiast has begun to practise these, the pleasure to be gained from quietly working a heavy horse – harrowing a field, carting around the farm, ploughing the land, or driving a dray or waggon – is immeasurably satisfying.

Finding the right working horse for one's particular needs is important. Special care must be taken to ensure a good temperament. The breed societies and the working horse associations are good places to start, but heavy horses can also be found at auctions or by word of mouth. Unless seeking a giant, the enthusiast should aim to purchase a horse of 16.2–17.2 hands (some Shires can reach 19 hands in height). Inexperienced people should begin with an older horse, already trained and adept in a variety of different types of work. It is also essential to find an adviser – someone who is already knowledgeable about heavy horses and who can point out the pitfalls.

Below left: Tom Sampson, who works in West Sussex, applying a hot shoe to the hoof of a Shire.

Below right: The vet's visit is an essential part of horse ownership: here a vet is monitoring the heartbeat of a horse during a cross-country trials event.

Heavy horses need access to good-quality grazing: 2 or 3 acres (0.8–1.2 hectares) are sufficient for one horse; 6 acres (2.4 hectares) will enable expansion to two horses at a later stage. As a heavy horse weighs nearly a ton (the average weight is 650–750 kg), substantial fencing is needed. Wire or electric fencing is acceptable, providing it is kept in good condition. Ideally the horse will also have access to a stable that is dry, well ventilated and free from draughts, no smaller than 12 by 14 feet (3.7 by 4.3 metres). Space is also needed to keep bedding, hay and feed, harness, grooming kit and medicines, which must be kept in a locked cupboard.

The average working horse needs very little 'hard' feed. If the horse is in light but regular general work, in addition to grass in the summer and hay in the winter, 6 pounds (2.7 kg) of rolled barley with chaff fed twice daily should be sufficient. Heavy horse owners should not be tempted by the vast array of specialist horse feeds available.

Heavy horses are, by and large, 'good doers' and, apart from the effects of mite infestation in those breeds with feather, usually do not suffer the many ailments affecting lighter horses. However, it is important to consider their well-being at all times and veterinary visits will be needed on occasion. They must be regularly wormed, receive annual equine flu injections and dental checks. Their legs and feet need special care because of the sheer weight they are expected to carry. Regular visits (usually six-weekly) from the farrier are essential to keep the hooves properly trimmed and shod if the horses are working on hard surfaces. This is not cheap: a single visit in 2004 cost around £100 to £120 for one horse.

Training for potential horsemen is available in a variety of different ways. There is no substitute for learning directly, one to one, from someone with real working horse experience, so cultivating a friendship with such a person is to be recommended. Bespoke training courses are also offered by individual horsemen on their farms, by breed societies and by working horse associations, which sometimes arrange special training

Training has become ever more important as those with career knowledge of the skills needed to work a heavy horse diminish in number. Specialist training courses are available in different parts of Britain. Here Cheryl Grover leads students through the process of harnessing up and hitching in.

days. Nationally recognised qualifications in working heavy horses are available along with separate Road Driving Assessments through the British Horse Society, and training in forestry work is organised through the Forestry Contracting Association.

In the case of a young horse needing training, again an adviser is invaluable: training a working horse is an exacting task. A young horse must be handled from birth, encouraged to be calm and quiet and familiarised with being led and having his legs picked up for hoof care. 'Breaking in' should begin at the age of two and a half or three years. An owner needs to build up a relationship with the horse and approach every stage gently. Harness should be introduced gradually, moving on to driving with a helper at his head and getting him used to the basic commands 'come here' to go left, 'walk off' to go right, 'whoa' to stop and 'get back' to go backwards (these commands vary slightly in different parts of Britain). At this stage the horse will be ready for a light load.

Once that is achieved the horse must learn to pull a shafted vehicle at the walk. Then loads in the cart should be introduced, first light and then building up in weight, and he should be taught to back the vehicle. Most important of all, he must learn to stand still. The horse will then be ready to meet a variety of different situations: tractors at work; lorries arriving; walking through puddles and streams; road signs; plastic bags and sacks on the ground. It will take time and a great deal of patience, but care taken at this stage will always be repaid.

Harness varied region by region during the heyday of the working horse and old sets can still be found. One of the most obvious variations is with the collar – horsemen in Scotland and northern England prefer 'high peaked' collars. Cross-country driving enthusiasts and smallholders favour the modern style of harness used in North America, which is cheaper and easier to care for. Nevertheless there is nothing to match a good-quality set of English leather harness, and these can still be obtained new.

Training a young horse – Nick Rayner introduces a light load, with a helper on an extra rein.

There are four basic types of harness – shaft (or cart), trace, plough and pair (or pole). Shaft harness consists of bridle, collar and hames, cart saddle or pad and a set of breechings. Most bridles include blinkers, introduced to restrict the horse's sight-line to a narrow forward and downward range. In the past there were hundreds of different designs of bit. In the twenty-first century these have largely narrowed down to a straight bar, ideal for agricultural work, and the Liverpool bit, a curbed driving bit that gives greater control over horses being driven on roads or in confined spaces, such as a show ring. The well-fitted padded collar holds the hames, making a rigid frame and providing a means of attaching the horse to its load. The cart saddle or pad takes some of the weight of a shafted vehicle on the horse's back via a ridger chain passed from one shaft to the other. This is held in position by a girth strap fixed under the belly of the horse and via a short 'meter' strap to the collar and a wide strap attached to the breeching. The breeching is the horse's braking system. Attached to the shafts by short chains, the breeching is used to hold back the cart, on a steep hill perhaps, or to reverse it.

Trace harness is used when horses are coupled in line, one in front of the other, and can be a useful hitch in confined spaces, such as in forests, to add extra horsepower or for interest in the show ring. The bridle, collar and hames are the same as for cart harness. Instead of a cart saddle a back band is used – a broad strip of leather with fittings to hold up the 12 foot (3.7 metre) trace chains and a crupper strap ending in a loop through which the horse's tail is drawn. A belly band is used to keep the collar below the horse's windpipe. Hip straps help keep the trace chains away from the horse's legs.

A Shire wearing shaft harness pulling the Cyril Knowles dray.

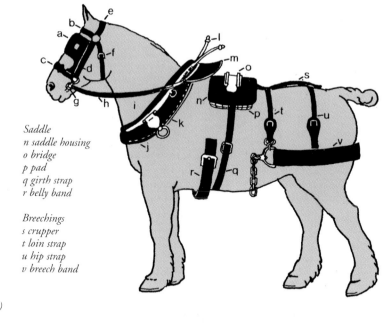

Shaft harness

Bridle
a *blinker*
b *brow band*
c *nose band*
d *cheek strap*
e *head strap*
f *throat lash*
g *bit*
h *bearing rein*

Collar
i *forewale*
j *side-piece*
k *body (the padding)*
l *hames*
m *housen*

Saddle
n *saddle housing*
o *bridge*
p *pad*
q *girth strap*
r *belly band*

Breechings
s *crupper*
t *loin strap*
u *hip strap*
v *breech band*

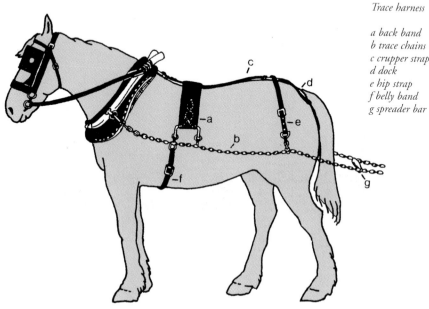

Trace harness

a *back band*
b *trace chains*
c *crupper strap*
d *dock*
e *hip strap*
f *belly band*
g *spreader bar*

Traditional harness, from 'The Heavy Horse: Its Harness and Harness Decoration' by Terry Keegan.

A Suffolk horse (Mr D. Wager's Blaxhall Blossom) wearing a fine set of class-winning shaft harness.

Plough harness is similar to trace harness and is used when working a pair of horses side by side. In place of the cart saddle is the plough band or back band, used to hold up the plough traces. Cotton plough lines are used to control the horses, and rope, leather or chain couplers to keep the horses together at the front.

Pair harness is used when hitching a pair of horses to the pole of a dray or trade vehicle. The cart saddle is replaced by a lightweight pad since its main function is to hold up the trace chains. There are ring terrets on the pad, through which the leather reins are threaded. Breechings are lighter as the job of braking the vehicle is taken over by a pair of pole chains from the front of the pole to the bottom chain of the hames. Braking is also controlled by the driver, who has a foot brake on the vehicle.

North American harness is distinguished chiefly by its use of a split collar and pad (much lighter and more flexible than the English version) and quarter straps from each side of the breechings, which go under the belly and clip on to a strap that runs between the horse's front legs and attaches to the neck yoke. This provides a very efficient braking system.

Left: Champion ploughman Charlie Coffen's plough horses, showing the coupling chains used to keep them together at the front.

Pair harness on Tom Brewster's Bandirran Clydesdale dray, showing the pole straps attached to the pole at the front.

Modern harness on David Baker's Percheron, showing the split collar and pad and the quarter straps beneath the belly that are favoured in North America.

Forestry horses usually use Scandinavian harness, designed specifically for the task of hauling timber out of woodland. The shafts of a timber arch or forwarder are much shorter than on a conventional wheeled vehicle and are fitted to a short strap from the collar and another strap from the light pad across the horse's back.

Fully harnessed, the horse is now ready to work an implement. A single horse is joined to, say, a harrow or roller by a whipple tree. Attached with a single chain to the implement, this holds the trace chains from either side of the horse: the crooks on the chains should always face upwards to avoid snagging on the ground. Where two horses are used two whipple trees will be needed, and for a larger team a set of eveners is necessary in order to 'even out' the amount of work done by each horse.

Accurate driving is important in field work so that no part of the field is missed in, for example, a harrowing or a drilling operation. The horseman should walk 3 to 4 feet (about 1 metre) behind the implement, but at one side to ensure good vision and straight lines.

Accuracy is also important when using a cart or waggon. The position of the vehicle in relation to the horse is crucial for the animal's comfort. When the horse has been hitched in, the end of the shafts should sit just below the hame hook. Traditionally carts and waggons would be driven

Bill Jarrett's plough horses, showing the arrangement of whipple trees between the horses and the implement.

from the ground, allowing the vehicle to be fully loaded. The horseman walks at the nearside of the horse, level with the rump. Backing is best done from the horse's head with the hands either side of the bit, guiding the horse back gently. Driven vehicles such as drays or cross-country driving vehicles are backed from the vehicle seat by gentle pressure on the reins.

The skill of ploughing is the zenith of a horseman's achievement. Champion ploughmen are capable of razor-sharp furrows, with all stubble buried and with ruler-straight 'openings' and 'finishes'. Match ploughing became popular in the nineteenth century and still attracts crowds at events throughout Britain. The two classes of ploughing usually seen in modern times are general-purpose and high-cut, also known as 'oat seed furrow'. General-purpose ploughing produces a more broken furrow that

can easily be harrowed down to form a seed bed. High-cut ploughing produces a furrow suitable for sowing seed by broadcasting over the furrows. The plough used has an extra-long mould-board, which turns the furrow slowly, ensuring that the soil remains unbroken. A typical plough plot measures 8 by 80 yards (7.3 by 73.2 metres).

Many people enjoy showing their horses at agricultural shows and events. There are classes for in-hand, turnout, harness decoration and riding. To turn out a horse to show standard involves careful preparation work and a great deal of time. In-hand showmen concentrate on the

Jim Elliott – one of the most successful modern ploughing champions – competes in a high-cut class (above), and (right) Wynne Hull from Lancashire finishes his general-purpose plot at a northern ploughing match.

Above: *A Shire performs his 'show' before the judge at the National Shire Horse Show.*

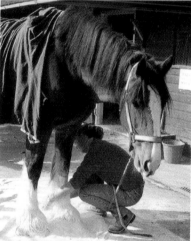

Right: *One of the Brookfield Shires team having his front feather washed out and dried with white sawdust.*

A Percheron's mane (below left) and a Suffolk's tail (below right) being plaited by braiding champions Matthew and Norma Bradley.

A show dray, fully dressed for showing, with nosebags and bucket.

conformation of their animals and their movement to ensure that they make a good 'show' in front of the judges. Turnout competitors must present not only fine horses but also perfectly clean harness and a spotless vehicle. Decorated harness devotees spend hours preparing their much-loved harness sets and the brass and sometimes floral decorations on which they will finally be judged.

Before a show horses are bathed and, in the case of Shires and Clydesdales, have their feather carefully cleaned and dried, leaving white silky hair. Tails and manes are plaited according to the traditions for the breed: the manes of Suffolks are always fully plaited while those of Shires, Clydesdales and Percherons have only a small proportion of the hair included. Both use raffia or wool to make the plait and 'flights' made of ribbon to stand out along the crest. Tail decoration is more varied but usually Suffolks and Percherons are fully plaited, while smaller plaits at the base of the dock are used for Shires and Clydesdales.

Harness must be black and buckles must be cleaned on the underside as well as the top; brass must be given a last-minute polish to ensure the best shine. Vehicles must be clean on the top and the underside, and must be 'dressed' with nosebags, water buckets and rope. The horseman must dress suitably in traditional jacket, shirt, tie and hat, which should be either bowler or cap.

Tradition is important in showing, but even here there is evolution. Increasingly, in the twenty-first century, classes are being held for ridden heavy horses and a debate has begun about the types of vehicle allowed in turnout classes. For all owners of heavy horses there is much to discover and enjoy – tasks to undertake; horses, vehicles, harness and brass to acquire; and skills to perfect.

Horsemen must be well dressed for showing. Here a tweed jacket, cap and leather gloves, twill trousers and country shirt and tie are ideal for driving a smart waggon in a parade.

Ploughing at Hurstbourne Tarrant, Hampshire.

Heavy horses in agriculture, forestry and trade

Heavy horses were once the linchpin of Britain's economy, especially the agricultural economy. They ploughed the soil; drilled the seed; cut, raked, turned and carted the hay; harvested the cereals with the binder and carted the stooks of corn to the rickyard. They hauled root crops, carted produce to market and took manure out to the fields to begin the whole process again for another year.

As the eminent draught-horse historian Keith Chivers has pointed out, the agricultural revolution of the eighteenth and nineteenth centuries would not have taken place but for the horse. The newly invented

Timber hauliers at work. Horses in pickaxe formation pull a timber carriage loaded with butts collected from the forest. Note the use of the roller scotch on chains behind the nearside back wheel as a brake on steep inclines.

Above: *Three teams of three horses drilling a field.*

Left: *Passing a newly thatched barn, horse teams are led out for their day's work.*

Below: *Horsemen pose with their Clydesdale work horses in Scotland. Note the traditional Scottish high-peaked collars, also popular in northern England.*

Building a mangel clamp – farm workers and a Percheron horse with a tip cart engaged in storing the vital fodder crop before winter sets in.

Horses at rest in a field at West Overton, Wiltshire.

machinery and equipment could not have been worked by the slower oxen, which had long been the mainstay of agriculture, nor by human labour. Much later, in the 1939 agricultural war effort, tractors were still regarded as supplementary to working horses.

But by the 1950s and 1960s the tractor and the motor lorry seemed a more attractive and progressive option. Machines needed less attention

Horses and a tractor working together in a field in Fotheringhay, Northamptonshire, in 1940.

Above: *Before horses finally replaced oxen the two were often worked side by side, especially in more remote places. This pair are reaping oats on a farm in Orkney.*

Left: *A small number of farmers still use horses on their land for most tasks. Geoff Morton of Holme upon Spalding Moor, East Yorkshire, did much to keep the skills of working horses alive in the 1960s, 1970s and 1980s. He was also among the first to offer training courses for those interested in learning how to use horses in agriculture. Here, he is using a team of six to prepare a seedbed with a trailed coil at Hasholme Carr Farm.*

and oil was cheap, tasks could be achieved faster, the labourer's toil appeared a thing of the past – the heavy horse's pivotal place on the land was at an end.

Some farmers remained unconvinced by the new technology, or simply preferred their horses. Their determination has left a legacy of knowledge to be passed on to younger people convinced that the horse has much to offer modern society. Working horse farmers – though small in number – are dedicated to concern for the environment, long-term care of the soil, retention of the immense skill of horsemanship, preservation of the heavy breeds for their own sake and the companionship that working with animals brings. Many of them continue to use the traditional implements and

Jonathan Waterer of Chittlehampton, Devon, another modern working horse farmer, drives his Shires from the harvest field after collecting sheaves of corn previously cut with a horse-drawn binder.

Joe Godderidge using his working horses on his farm near Dereham, Norfolk.

vehicles familiar to their fathers and grandfathers, but there is a growing interest in manufacturing modern horse-drawn equipment for today's needs. Some equipment has been imported from American and Canadian Amish farmers, and implements designed for all-terrain vehicles (ATVs) can be adapted for horse use. One entrepreneur has designed a range of equipment including hitch carts with power take-off (pto), which are in demand in Britain and Europe.

Strong draught horses had been essential in forestry and the timber trade. In the deciduous forests of Britain they were employed in large

Charlie Pinney using his self-designed Pintow Power Cart with mounted finger-bar mower.

Horse logger Rob Rawstorne using his mare to clear 180 tonnes of timber at North West Water's Rivington Estate, Lancashire, in 2000.

numbers and big teams were used to haul mature hardwoods out to the roads and railways and on to the sawmills. Timber carriages were extendable to cater for different lengths of timber, and huge two-wheeled timber arches were used in the woods to transport larger butts from the felling sites. The introduction of machinery had the same effect on the horse in the forests as it had on the farms and in the towns.

However, in the 1980s there was a sudden revival of horse use in forestry. Environmental considerations in sensitive woodland where flora and fauna must be preserved led to a technical study by the Forestry Authority that

Devon horse logger Colette Meade using her Ardennes horse to extract hardwood with a modern Scandinavian -made timber arch.

showed that the use of horses could be more effective and economic in certain circumstances. Heavily influenced by Scandinavian horse-logging techniques and equipment, British horse loggers found their skills were in demand by private woodland owners and organisations such as Forest Enterprise and the National Trust. Wiltshire farmers Richard and Angela Gifford were instrumental in promoting horses for forestry work. In 2004 there were around forty loggers working in Britain.

Smaller draught horses are in demand for logging, along with new equipment, including timber arches and forwarders and special harness, often imported from Sweden and Norway. Training in horse logging is available, alongside forestry training, through the Forestry Contracting Association based in Aberdeenshire. Modern horse-logging work practices have been established, and some loggers work their horses in conjunction with modern machines to achieve the most economic result.

One logger has designed a completely new range of implements for work in countryside conservation projects, including a bracken-basher and the heathland rehabilitation harrow suitable for use over recently cleared woodland. These implements have been used behind horses in areas where bracken needs to be cleared and where the ground is being prepared for a resurgence of traditional heather.

Alongside the agricultural revolution came the industrial revolution, bringing with it the construction of railways and canals, the extension of mining and quarrying and a vast increase in manufactured goods. All these industries were entirely dependent on the horse for transport and

Railways, mills, mines, quarries, docks and warehouses were kept in business through the use of the draught horse. Loads moved by horses at Liverpool Docks, for example, were diverse and heavy. This photograph was taken at the Pier Head, Liverpool, in 1946. (From left) The first load is forty bales of Sudan cotton, weighing 7 tons; the second load, also weighing 7 tons, is Irish bacon; the third load is dried fruit. Two other horse-drawn vehicles are in front of this, one empty, having delivered its load, and the other with an unidentified load. The horses were servicing the ships but when container ships took over they were no longer needed in the port.

*Liverpool
Corporation horses
Vedas and Vulcan,
who stood just over
16 hands, were
engaged in pulling
tests in London in
1924. Note their
relatively short legs
and deep bodies,
ideal for draught.
These two were
pictured in the
1925 Shire Horse
Society stud book.*

distribution. The horse's role was almost forgotten in the excitement of new forms of power but its legacy has lived on in terms such as 'horsepower', used to measure the power of engines.

Nowhere is the role of the horse just before the introduction of petrol-driven vehicles better exemplified than in Liverpool. Here vast numbers of horses were stabled by transport companies serving the docks and warehouses of this city. Tales of extraordinary loads, carters' determination in the face of Second World War bombing and horsemen's pride in their equine charges abound. So strong is the bond between former carters in the city that they formed a group to fight for a permanent sculpture commemorating the work of the horse in Liverpool.

Real draught-horse use in towns has dwindled to a few enthusiastic brewing companies who continue to use horses to deliver beer in inner cities. The dray horse is celebrated throughout the United Kingdom by showmen who compete in turnout classes with their brewers' drays or commercial vehicles and horses whose ancestors worked a full day, from early in the morning, six days a week, with consequently short lives.

Just as the few heavy horse breeders still at work in the 1950s and 1960s saved the breeds as we know them from extinction, so those few farmers and foresters using horses commercially in the twenty-first century are keeping alive essential skills. Who knows when they will be needed in the future?

Charlie Pinney, who farms in Wales, says the draught horse should be recognised as a 'self-replicating energy source whose ecological and economic benefits have been neglected for too long'. For small-scale operations the draught horse was cost-effective, efficient and economic. 'Real living horse power is complementary to organic farming philosophy, concern for the environment, reduced reliance on fossil fuels, zero pollution and all the other agri-business arguments.'

The yard at Young's Brewery in Wandsworth, London, in 1896, when horse-drawn deliveries were at their peak.

Marketing, promotion and leisure

The magnificence of heavy horses at their best, perfectly turned out with coats shining and silky feather flying, jet-black leather harness and polished brass gleaming, ensured their use as a promotional tool in the image-conscious last third of the twentieth century.

The breweries, which had played such an important role in helping ensure the survival of the heavy horse in the 1950s and 1960s, led the way in marketing products with the use of a finely tuned pair of heavy draught horses drawing a freshly painted brewer's dray. They were present at pub openings and beer launches, and, taking the message to as

Vaux Brewery's Percheron horses delivering beer in the centre of Sunderland in the 1990s, a much scaled-down operation compared to the days when the brewery was at full stretch. In 1904, soon after the first steam engines were introduced to supplement the horses, the company employed 120 Shires, Clydesdales and Cleveland Bays. The brewery closed in 1999 and the heavy horse operation was sold.

Kevin Flynn drives a pickaxe, three horses in the lead, two in the 'wheel', to a Young's Brewery dray during the London Harness Horse Parade.

wide an audience as possible, also at agricultural shows, parades and events.

The top brewery teams, Young's, Whitbread, Tetley and Samuel Smith, for example, were the turnouts to beat in the show ring and had the resources to parade the biggest teams and most unusual hitches, such as the unicorn (a pair on the pole and a single horse in front) and the pickaxe (a single in shafts and a pair in front). In 1998 Young's head horseman Kevin Flynn entered the London Harness Horse Parade at Battersea Park, London, with four in line representing each of the main British breeds of heavy horse, Shire, Clydesdale, Suffolk and British Percheron.

In the 1970s and 1980s new professional heavy horse businesses contracted their teams to appear for large companies, notably Brookfield Shires of Huntingdon, Cambridgeshire, who promoted Galliford PLC and

John Peacock of Lingwood Shires was one of those who developed a business around the promotional use of heavy horses. For many years he drove his Shires and the Ind Coope brewer's dray and he continues to participate in shows and events across Britain.

High-profile events keep the public interested in heavy horses. Colin Horler took the world record for driving a team of twenty Shires at the Bath and West Showground in 1991.

Tarmac, for example, and John Peacock's Lingwood Shires of Brentwood, Essex, who undertook a wide range of promotions including, for many years, the brewers Ind Coope. Later John Peacock was largely responsible for drawing up the heavy horse elements of the Road Driving Assessment test, sought as a qualification by public authorities as evidence of high standards in horsemanship.

By the end of the twentieth century brewery involvement with heavy horses was diminishing as new marketing officers concentrated on other ways of promoting their products. Whitbread's greys, famous for half a century, were sold, along with the company's hop farm in Kent, which became a leisure attraction. A few of the greys continued alongside Radford Shires' blacks at the Hop Farm Country Park in the care of Colin Horler. Smaller brewers have continued their support, however. Badger

Randy Hiscock driving two of his team of four Suffolk mares to the Badger Brewery dray.

Horses have made a comeback in the streets of towns and cities, where they are often used for tasks in parks and gardens or in town centres, as here, watering hanging baskets in Halifax. The horses were provided by Horses at Work, now based at Bradford Industrial Museum.

Brewery of Blandford St Mary, Dorset, has linked up with Randy Hiscock of Shaftesbury, who drives a team of four Suffolk mares – one of only two four-horse teams of Suffolks in Britain – to promote their products.

In the early 1980s local authorities recognised the impact heavy horses could have on the public image of some of their services. Aberdeen led the way, with its director of leisure and recreation, David Welch, introducing Clydesdales for a range of tasks previously achieved using lorries and vans. In December 1980 Welch bought two Clydesdales to replace a 35 cwt (1587.6 kg) van: by 1987 the council owned thirty-eight horses including working geldings and mares producing foals, which brought in extra income. They were used in a stagecoach service, parks transport, on civic occasions and for collecting autumn leaves. In 1983 David Welch pointed out that two six-year-old Clydesdales together with their harness and a cart cost £5500 and £7800 respectively to run. A van cost £7200, with a further £8500 in running costs. Its life was seven years, shorter than that of a horse, and harness and carts generally went up in value. 'There are advantages in introducing horses besides utility and economy,' he said. 'There is the question of civic cheerfulness. Nothing is quite so agreeable to the eye as a pair of large horses and a cart, their amiability in sharp distinction to the menace and aggression of the motor car. Their hooves make a cheerful rhythmical clatter, and the iron-shod wheels of the cart grate with a continuous burr upon the carriageway like the drone of a bagpipe. They elicit smiles from adults and waves from children.'

Other authorities followed suit – Glasgow, Manchester, Leeds, Dartford, Gillingham, Hillingdon, Chesterfield and Birmingham. In the late 1990s Bracknell Forest Borough Council introduced fresh roles for the local authority horse. In the shadow of towering modern office blocks

One of the local authorities most committed to the use of horses is Bracknell Forest Borough Council. In addition to many tasks in and around the town centre the horses visit local schools, promoting the council and the cause of heavy horses at the same time.

The horse-drawn recycling project for Bath and North East Somerset Council is organised in partnership with Avon Friends of the Earth. Driving the Percheron horse in the shafts of the modern vehicle specially built for the purpose is Ian Judge, project supervisor. This service began in 1997.

and factories, horses were used to draw gang mowers in the council's parks and gardens, as well as for the more usual tasks of rubbish clearance and watering hanging baskets in the town centre. In addition Bracknell fitted out its horse-drawn passenger waggon with a lift to enable disabled people to enjoy the service.

Bath and North East Somerset Council introduced a recycling service using Percheron horses. Other local authorities contract local horsemen and their teams to undertake certain tasks on certain days. In Stratford-upon-Avon, for example, a horse bus, drawn by Percherons, operated during the main summer season. In his later post as chief executive of the Royal Parks, David Welch kept faith with his belief in horses and introduced them into Richmond and Bushy Parks, where they undertake a range of tasks including harrowing the rides.

The best advocates of heavy horses are their owners. They market them directly to the public in showing classes – in-hand and turnout – at agricultural shows throughout the United Kingdom. Showing is a magnet

Above: *A trade turnout class underway at the Essex Heavy Horse Show in 1999. Participation in such classes gave exposure to sponsoring breweries and other companies while helping keep the heavy horse driving tradition alive.*

Coalite produced one of the most spectacular champion turnouts of modern times during the late 1980s with a partnership between horseman and driver Laurie Whittle and the Shire gelding Vincent. Vincent was eventually exported to the United States. In the photograph he is taking part in the East of England Show, 1990.

Above left: *The traditional Easter Monday London Harness Horse Parade has been a showcase for driven equines since 1885. Now taking place at Battersea Park, London, the original purpose of the parade – to ensure a high standard of care in working horses – is less necessary than in the days when everything was moved by horse. Nevertheless participants are still expected to perform to a very high standard; to do any less results in a second-class certificate. This photograph shows a half-bred heavy drawing a highly attractive florist's trolley.*

Above right: *Portsmouth Parade is the largest modern heavy horse parade in the United Kingdom. Started in 1984 by Mike Millington, who horses the heavy horse turnout for the brewers George Gale & Co, based at Horndean in Hampshire, and show commentator John 'Jumbo' Lovatt, it attracts some fifty turnouts from all over Britain for a two-day festival on Southsea Common, Hampshire.*

Decorated horse classes were an important part of shows and parades. Horsemen would delight in showing off their skills in decorating their horse and its harness with highly polished harness and brasses, traditional flowers, ribbons and wool. The photograph on the left shows a line-up of Shires decorated for a parade, probably in Liverpool. A few shows still run classes: the horse below left was photographed at the National Shire Horse Show, Peterborough. Below right is another, more restrained, example, Wellington, a Shire owned by the Coors Visitor Centre, with head horseman Barry Coffen.

Several horsemen keep the tradition of agricultural turnout classes alive, offering the public the opportunity to see magnificent regional waggons in use. This is Gwylim Evans with his Percheron, Louise, drawing an Aylesbury road waggon built by J. Plater of Haddenham, Buckinghamshire.

not just for the traditional heavy horse breeders but for new owners too, as a pastime in its own right. Agricultural shows provided an important testing ground for breed lines in the past, with results having a direct effect on breeding conformation trends. This is still the case in the twenty-first century, although the markets for animals are different and are geared towards leisure rather than agricultural work.

Some shows serve as qualifiers for regional or national competitions, such as the West of England Heavy Horse Championship and the Shire Horse of the Year Championship. Enthusiasts enjoy taking part in other specialist events, such as the heavy horse parades in Portsmouth and Liverpool (revived from the 1930s and 1940s) or at local fairs and carnivals, and frequently find their horses and waggons in demand for weddings and funerals.

Workings, where horses demonstrate non-competitively their skills at traditional and modern tasks, have become a favourite activity, both for horsemen and the public – a way of gathering together informally and enjoyably with like-minded folk. The atmosphere rubs off on visitors, including people who have worked with horses in their youth.

The emphasis on leisure as a market and the reduction of their traditional work has led to new activities for heavy horses. Obstacle driving, in which pairs of horses are driven through a course marked with cones, was introduced in the 1980s, following rules similar to those for light horses. Another activity is the newer sport of cross-country trials. Introduced in 1995, this involves dressage, a marathon, a course of hazards and a cone-driving course. Followers of the sport comprised the first wholly British team in the international La Route du Poisson in France (1999), in which pairs of heavy draught horses race in a twenty-seven-hour relay from Boulogne to Paris, retracing the traditional route of fresh fish rushed by horse-drawn vehicles from the coast to city restaurants. In 2002 the first British heavy horse team relay race, the New Forest Beer Run, took place in Hampshire, run along similar lines.

'Workings', where horsemen get together on a farm in their region to demonstrate agricultural tasks and the leisure use of their animals, have become increasingly popular, organised through a network of working horse associations. (Below) A traditional timber 'bob' or 'jigger wheels' being demonstrated with an oak log at an event at the Weald & Downland Open Air Museum, West Sussex. (Centre left) Rob Dash and his Shire pair using a furrow press at a Hampshire working. (Centre right) A Clydesdale rowing up hay at a working at the Museum of Scottish Rural Life in Wester Kittochside. (Bottom) Randy Hiscock's four Suffolks drawing a seed drill at a Southern Counties Heavy Horse Association working.

Robert Sampson with an eighteen-horse hitch of Percherons on his farm at Harbridge, Hampshire.

Right: *Bob Hill demonstrating the use of a horse-drawn binder at a working in Devon.*

The sport of heavy horse cross-country driving is becoming increasingly popular after its introduction in the south of England. As well as driving trials events throughout the south, a British team competes in the international La Route du Poisson in France – held to celebrate and promote draught horses in Europe. In the photograph John McDermott, co-founder of the cross-country driving club, with his wife, Rowena, drives his Percheron pair through a water hazard during a cross-country event in Hampshire in 2000.

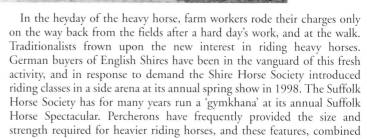

Horsemen riding home astride their Percherons at the end of a day's work at Weston, Somerset, in 1934.

In the heyday of the heavy horse, farm workers rode their charges only on the way back from the fields after a hard day's work, and at the walk. Traditionalists frown upon the new interest in riding heavy horses. German buyers of English Shires have been in the vanguard of this fresh activity, and in response to demand the Shire Horse Society introduced riding classes in a side arena at its annual spring show in 1998. The Suffolk Horse Society has for many years run a 'gymkhana' at its annual Suffolk Horse Spectacular. Percherons have frequently provided the size and strength required for heavier riding horses, and these features, combined with their relative agility, good temperament and lack of feather, have made them popular as the foundation for police horses. Many miles from their traditional homeland, Clydesdales have even been raced in Japan.

Riding heavy horses for leisure has become increasingly popular. Here Niki Stephen is astride three-year-old Clydesdale Arradoul Sabrina at the Aberdeen Clydesdale Show in August 2001. Sabrina is by Clydesdale stallion Collessie Cut Above, pictured on page 13. The horse was broken to ride by Niki's sister Philly.

A farrier at work on the feet of a cart-horse outside a picturesque forge.

The heavy horse industry and the revival years

Servicing heavy horses to ensure that the wheels of commerce and agriculture kept turning was a thriving industry employing many people in town and countryside in the past. From vets and farriers, through harness-makers, smiths and wheelwrights to the manufacturers of agricultural implements, all had a vital role to play in the economy.

In the twenty-first century this industry is much constricted, but it is still possible to order a new set of traditional English leather harness and to find a wheelwright able to build or restore a waggon. Many of these tradesmen have adapted to the new demands as well. Modern handmade webbing harness is popular with horse farmers and cross-country trials enthusiasts: it is substantially cheaper than leather and can be cleaned in the washing machine. Cross-country trials vehicles are made by some wheelwrights, as well as by new companies established to service the larger carriage-driving market.

Brass and chrome fittings for heavy horse harness, trace and tug chains, mane and tail decorations, plough lines and halters are all still available, mainly through The Heavy Horse Enthusiast business, established in the 1970s to service horsemen's needs. However, some traditional fittings are increasingly unavailable or on the brink of disappearance. It is impossible

Left: *An advertisement for horseshoes made by Benjamin Baker (Lye) Ltd of Stourbridge, Worcestershire.*

Above: *Shropshire harness-maker Terry Davis making a traditional English horse collar. The 'wale' or body of the collar is stuffed with rye straw grown to order for the purpose.*

A wheelwright fitting felloes to a wheel in his workshop at Fawley in Herefordshire c.1937.

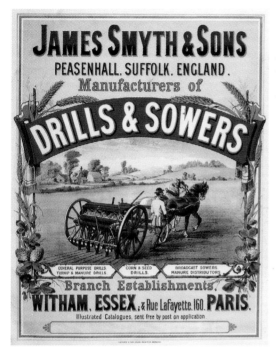

Catalogues promoted the diverse products of manufacturers of agricultural implements in the heyday of the working horse. Here are pages from the catalogues of two prominent makers, James Smyth & Sons, whose drills were eagerly sought by farmers, and Ransomes, Sims & Jefferies Ltd, whose ploughs are even now the most sought after by ploughing match competitors.

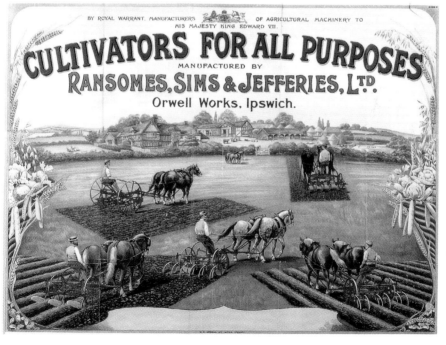

Rye straw being harvested at the Weald & Downland Open Air Museum, West Sussex, ready for distribution to harness-makers.

Right: *Hampshire wheelwright Keith Randall fitting iron strakes to a wheel destined for a replica medieval cart scaled off the fourteenth-century Luttrell Psalter for the Weald & Downland Open Air Museum's medieval farmstead project.*

A modern cross-country trials vehicle and modern webbing harness in use on the New Forest Beer Run, 2002.

Mane and tail decorations, such as these 'flights' used on one of Paul and Walt Bedford's Shires, are available along with other heavy horse harness accessories through small businesses set up for the purpose, for example The Heavy Horse Enthusiast.

to obtain new cased hames (in which a wooden former is encased in sheet iron and covered with brass): its modern counterpart is made from cast aluminium-bronze and is heavier than the original. The popular Yorkshire halters, ideal for comfort beneath a leather bridle, could no longer be bought in 2004 and attempts are being made to design a modern equivalent. The distinctive blue and white chequered collar cloth, used to line horses' collars, ceased manufacture in 1999, but Bradford Industrial Museum is using its historic textile machinery to make it again. Quality rye straw for stuffing collars has to be grown to order for a group of harness-makers.

Many horse farmers and loggers use traditional implements adapted for modern use – hay rakes, mowers, harrows, for example. But there is a

New and second-hand harness is available at specialist auctions or heavy horse workings: this range is on Amanda Peters's stand in Hampshire.

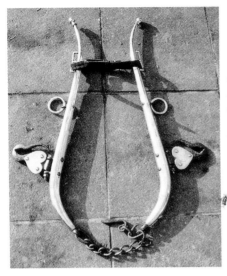

Cased hames – no longer obtainable new following the demise of the traditional method of manufacture and a decrease in demand.

demand for modern equipment. Machines such as manure spreaders have been imported by their American Amish makers. In Britain Charlie Pinney's powered hitch carts can be used in conjunction with tractor-adapted equipment. Other farmers use implements originally made for use behind all-terrain vehicles, now popular as all-purpose transporters on modern farms.

Farriers continue to make a good living, but mostly from light horses used for leisure. Some refuse to shoe heavy horses because of the longer time and harder work involved, resulting in a dearth of suitable farriers in some areas. Vets increasingly have less experience of heavy horses,

In the early 1980s a historically significant display took place at the Suffolk Show to demonstrate a wide range of modern horse-drawn machinery. The event aimed to promote the use of the working horse in modern times. Here, Tom Walne drives a Suffolk to a fertiliser spreader.

Hitch carts enable tractor-designed agricultural implements to be pulled by horses. This example was designed by Nick Rayner of the New Forest, Hampshire, to his own specification.

and in the early twenty-first century many large-animal vets switched to small-animal practice, more lucrative and in greater demand. They are also influenced by the effect on livestock farmers of a series of health scares, such as the Bovine Spongiform Encephalopathy (BSE) crisis of the 1990s and the foot-and-mouth epidemic of 2001, with the resulting reduction in cattle, sheep and pig farming. Horse owners are forced to use specialist horse vets, who

Modern machinery for traditional tasks. (Top) Charlie Pinney with his pair-horse hitch cart and a pto-driven swath-turner attending to a hay crop in Argyll, Scotland. (Above) David Baker and his team of four black Percherons ploughing with an American 'sulky' plough imported from its Amish makers. (Left) Andy Musgrove and his Percheron pair demonstrating a machine of his own invention, a hydraulic-powered timber loader. (Below) The Working Horse Trust's pair of Ardennes drawing a powered hitch cart and a modern fertiliser spreader.

may have to travel large distances to make home visits.

By the 1980s concern was mounting about the future of the heavy horse. The Shire had the numerical advantage and marketing edge, and so it was the Shire Horse Society that initiated an investigation into the future of all the heavy breeds in 1985. With sponsorship from the Royal Agricultural Society of England (RASE) and led by Keith Chivers, the survey *History with a Future: Harnessing the Heavy Horse for the 21st Century* gathered seventy-six people representing all aspects of the heavy horse scene and all breeds in ten different study groups to consider new ideas for working and promoting heavy horses.

The project resulted in positive encouragement for a number of different areas, including promoting obstacle driving as a sport and advocating new leisure uses; demonstrating modern horse-drawn equipment; supporting greater use of horses in forestry and on small modern farms; encouraging the use of horses in short-haul, stop-start work in urban situations; and communicating the heritage of the heavy horse. 'The heavy horse has played a wider variety of vital roles in our history than any other animal or thing,' wrote Keith Chivers.

Meanwhile, out in the countryside all over England and, to a lesser extent, Scotland, Wales and Northern Ireland, heavy horse enthusiasts were taking matters into their own hands. In 1971 a small group of heavy horse enthusiasts anxious to preserve and promote the skill of horse ploughing met in Bramley Village Hall, Surrey. They formed the Southern Counties Heavy Horse Association (SCHHA), drawing up rules for ploughing matches, with the guidance of champion ploughman Jack Pearce. SCHHA holds the annual Great All England Ploughing Match and Heavy Horse Show in October, with a smaller spring working held in April. This was the first of a network of regional working societies formed to provide opportunities for people to get together to work their horses and demonstrate their skills for the benefit of themselves and the public.

Shire geldings owned by Mrs Cherryman of Chiddingfold, Surrey, with ploughman Tommy Gibson at a Surrey County Ploughing Match in 1975, in the early days of the revival.

Gathering the hay in the traditional way at the Weald & Downland Open Air Museum, Singleton, West Sussex.

Peter Brassett, head horseman at Beamish, North of England Open Air Museum, County Durham, with a Clydesdale in a tip cart working in the recreated 1820s landscape around the museum's restored Pockerley Manor.

Ploughing matches evoke the spirit of an earlier age: here genial competitiveness reigns at a Southern Counties Heavy Horse Association event.

By the late 1990s the network had become an established part of the heavy horse scene.

In the 1970s and 1980s visitors flocked to see the magnificent heavy horses put through their paces at matches, workings, events and parades. Interest in the heavy horse heritage was at its peak and had led to the formation of a number of heavy horse centres, notably the National Shire Horse Centre near Plymouth. Rare-breeds centres and working farms also included heavy horses among their attractions. Museums such as the Acton Scott Historic Working Farm, Roots of Norfolk at Gressenhall, Horses at Work at Bradford Industrial Museum, Beamish – the North of England Open Air Museum and the Weald & Downland Open Air Museum, West Sussex, used working horses to demonstrate agricultural and urban tasks from an era that, with every passing generation, was fast disappearing from memory.

The diverse and geographically widespread nature of heavy horses and their service industries makes the shows and events vital occasions at which to gather information and exchange ideas. In England there is no single more important occasion than the National Shire Horse Show, held annually in March on the East of England Showground at Peterborough. Here is the opportunity for chat at the ringside, the chance to

Getting up close to the horses as they are being prepared for a show, match or parade is a very popular activity with the public and has helped enormously in promoting the qualities of the heavy horse.

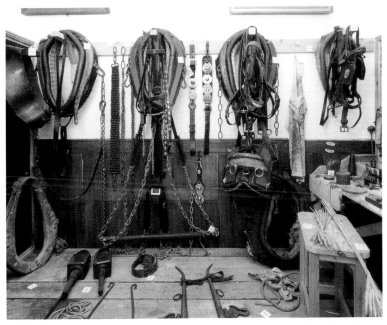

Traditional harness used on Suffolk Punches displayed in the Suffolk Punch Horse Museum in Woodbridge, Suffolk, headquarters of the breed's society.

Canal horses once ensured the success of the canal network, towing narrowboats from the towpaths adjacent to the canal. With specialist work methods and harness, reflecting the gaily coloured canal art found on the narrowboats, the canal horseman was highly skilled. Today horses are used on some canals to pull boats for the leisure industry, such as this one on the Llangollen Canal.

*Time for chat
and gossip –
preparing to
go into the
ring at the
National
Shire Horse
Show.*

visit trade stands of harness-makers and fittings suppliers, purchase the
latest heavy horse magazines, books and videos, meet enthusiasts from
overseas, and catch up with the latest gossip on heavy horse breeding and
conformation. It is also the first event of the season at which to meet
supporters of other breeds – the Clydesdale, the Suffolk and the British
Percheron – many will be helping their Shire-owning friends prepare for
classes.

As the twenty-first century began, and despite agricultural gloom and
mixed prices at horse sales, the heavy horse sector appeared relatively

*The Shire foal show
and sales at the end of
the season are an
important part of the
heavy horse calendar –
an opportunity for a
final look at stock
before the winter sets
in. Mark Richardson
shows Barrowshaw
Betsy to first place in
the two-year-old class
at the York Sales in
2001.*

Keen eyes watch the stallion parade at the Shire Horse Show, 2002.

buoyant. New enthusiasts were being attracted to buy, work and show heavy horses; fresh sport and leisure activities had been introduced and there was a small but sound movement using heavy horses in forestry and farming situations, especially where environmental considerations were high.

The foot-and-mouth epidemic of 2001 was to damage many farmers irreparably. While horses themselves were unaffected, their owners were badly hit; agricultural shows were cancelled and tourism enterprises closed. The following year, however, the champions of heavy horses were back in line, at work and on show. After the grim years of the 1950s and 1960s, when some breeds had come close to extinction, those who worked with heavy horses were more determined than ever in their resolve not to allow disaster to get the better of them.

Further information

Books

Baird, Eric. *The Clydesdale Horse*. Batsford, 1982.

Brigden, Roy. *Ploughs and Ploughing*. Shire, 1984; reprinted 2003.

Chivers, Keith. *The Shire Horse*. J. A. Allen, 1977.

Chivers, Keith. *History with a Future: Harnessing the Heavy Horse for the 21st Century*. Shire Horse Society/Royal Agricultural Society of England, 1988.

Chivers, Keith. *The Four Oaks*. The Lutterworth Press, 1994.

Evans, George Ewart. *The Horse in the Furrow*. Faber & Faber, 1960.

Hart, Edward. *The Care and Showing of Heavy Horses*. Batsford, 1981.

Hart, Edward. *Horse Drawn Farm Implements*. Japonica Press, 2003.

Hart, Edward. *Showing the Heavy Horse: An Exhibitor's Guide*. J. A. Allen, 2004.

Heiney, Paul. *Pulling Punches*. Methuen, 1988.

Keegan, Terry. *The Heavy Horse: Its Harness and Harness Decoration*. Pelham Books, 1973.

Russell, Valerie. *Heavy Horses of the World*. Country Life, 1983.

Sidbäck, Hans. *The Horse in the Forest*. Swedish University of Agricultural Sciences, 1993 (English translation).

Smith, D. J. *Discovering Horse-Drawn Farm Machinery*. Shire, second edition 1984; reprinted 1996.

Telleen, Maurice. *Draft Horse Primer*. Rodale Books, Emmaus, PA, USA, 1977.

Zeuner, Diana (editor). *The Working Horse Manual*. Old Pond Publishing/Heavy Horse World, 1998.

Magazines

Heavy Horse World Magazine, Lindford Cottage, Church Lane, Cocking, Midhurst, West Sussex GU29 0HW. Telephone: 01730 812419. Email: heavyhorse@mistral.co.uk. Website: www.heavyhorseworld.co.uk

Draft Horse Journal, PO Box 670, Waverley, IA 50677, USA.

Rural Heritage, 281 Dean Ridge Lane, Gainesboro, TN 38562-5039, USA.

Videos

A comprehensive selection of videos on heavy horse subjects can be obtained through *Heavy Horse World Magazine*, address as above.

Breed societies

Ardennes Horse Society of Great Britain, Jo Hewitt, Secretary, White Ash Farm, Starvenden Lane, Sissinghurst, Kent TN17 2AN. Telephone: 01580 715001.

British Percheron Horse Society, Muriel Bond, Secretary, Three Bears Cottage, Burston Road, Gissing, Diss, Norfolk IP22 5UF. Telephone: 01379 740554. Email: muriel@bond7675.freeserve.co.uk Website: www.percheron.org.uk

Clydesdale Horse Society, Mrs Marguerite Osborne MA LLB, Secretary, Kinclune, Kirriemuir, Angus DD8 5HX. Telephone: 01575 570900. Website: www.clydesdalehorsesociety.com

Shire Horse Society, Andrew Mercer, Secretary, East of England Showground, Peterborough PE2 6XE. Telephone: 01733 234451. Email: info@eastofengland.org.uk. Website: www.shire-horse.org.uk

Suffolk Horse Society, Amanda Hillier, Secretary, The Market Hill, Woodbridge, Suffolk IP12 4LU. Telephone: 01394 380643. Email: sec@suffolkhorsesociety.org.uk. Website: www.suffolkhorsesociety.org.uk

Where to see heavy horses

In addition to the following selection of attractions open to the public, heavy horses can be seen at country shows throughout Britain and workings, events and ploughing matches organised by working horse associations. Courses offering training in horsemanship are also available in different parts of Britain. For information contact *Heavy Horse World Magazine* (details on page 62).

Acton Scott Historic Working Farm, Wenlock Lodge, Acton Scott, Church Stretton, Shropshire SY6 6QN. Telephone: 01694 781306. Website: www.shropshireonline.gov.uk

Banham Zoo, The Grove, Banham, Norfolk NR16 2HE. Telephone: 01953 887771. Website: www.banhamzoo.co.uk

Beamish, North of England Open Air Museum, Stanley, County Durham DH9 0RG. Telephone: 0191 370 4000. Website: www.beamish.org.uk

Coors Visitor Centre, Horninglow Street, Burton upon Trent, Staffordshire DE14 1YQ. Telephone: 0845 600 0598. Website: www.bass-museum.com

Easton Farm Park, Easton, near Woodbridge, Suffolk IP13 0EQ. Telephone: 01728 746475. Website: www.eastonfarmpark.co.uk

Farming World, Nash Court, Boughton, Faversham, Kent ME13 9SW. Telephone: 01227 751144.

Hop Farm Country Park, Paddock Wood, Kent TN12 6PY. Telephone: 01622 872068. Website: www.thehopfarm.co.uk

Horses at Work, Bradford Industrial Museum, Moorside Mills, Moorside Road, Eccleshill, Bradford BD2 3HP. Telephone: 01274 631756. Website: www.bradford.gov.uk

Ironbridge Gorge Museum Trust, Ironbridge, Telford, Shropshire TF8 7AW. Telephone: 01952 433522. Website: www.ironbridge.org.uk

Norfolk Shire Horse Centre, West Runton, near Cromer, Norfolk NR27 9QH. Telephone: 01263 837339. Website: www.norfolk-shirehorse-centre-co.uk

Roots of Norfolk, Norfolk Rural Life Museum, Gressenhall, near Dereham, Norfolk NR20 4DR. Telephone: 01362 860563. Website: www.norfolk.gov.uk

Shires Family Adventure Park, Tredinnick, Wadebridge, Cornwall PL27 7RA. Telephone: 01841 541215. Website: www.shirespark.co.uk

Shire Horse Farm and Carriage Museum, Lower Gryllis Farm, Treskillard, Redruth, Cornwall TR16 6LA. Telephone: 01209 713606.

Stratford Shire Horse Centre, Clifford Road, Stratford-upon-Avon, Warwickshire CV37 8HW. Telephone: 01789 415274. Website: www.shirehorsecentre.co.uk

Suffolk Punch Heavy Horse Museum, The Market Hill, Woodbridge, Suffolk IP12 4LU. Telephone: 01394 380643. Website: www.suffolkhorsesociety.org.uk (No horses on show, but an extensive collection of artefacts.)

Weald & Downland Open Air Museum, Singleton, near Chichester, West Sussex PO18 0EU. Telephone: 01243 811363. Website: www.wealddown.co.uk

Working Horse Trust, Forge Wood Farm, Eridge Green, Tunbridge Wells TN3 9JT. Telephone: 01892 750105. Website: www.users.zetnet.co.uk/clivan/heavyhorses

Index